Second Edition August 2017

ISBN:1533469679
ISBN-13:9781533469670

i

DEDICATION

This is dedicated to the one I love.

JESUS, FATHER, SPIRIT

Celebrate World Turtle Day!!! May 23rd

I am passionate about art and about Sea Turtles, among other things. This book is to showcase these.

ACKNOWLEDGMENTS

I acknowledge that I am like a tree of life planted
by the living waters, bearing good fruit in every season.

Healthy Coral Reef

Sea Turtle Life

Written and Illustrated by

Deana G. Harvey

There is a lot to see in the deep blue sea. Sea Turtles get to enjoy a lot of beauty and intrigue as they travel the currents of the global waters. Flamey, Fire wrasse are little and fast-swimming fish living in coral reefs. Look! a blue tang. Sea Turtles like coral reefs and you can watch u-tube videos[1] of them searching for crabs and organisms. Sea Stars come in so many colors and red coral (seen in this detail) is endangered, as well as all sea turtles.

The 7 kinds of sea turtles are:

1. Leatherback Turtle
2. Kemp's Ridley Turtle
3. Olive Ridley Turtle
4. Green Turtle
5. Hawksbill Turtle
6. Loggerhead Turtle
7. Flatback Turtle

Read on for their different characteristics.

---

[1] Julie Seuss Photography on Face Book

Look ma! zero-gravity. Sea turtles live in a zero-gravity environment and they are buoyant. They can cut through the water with ease.

"I feel like I'm floating on air."

Zero Gravity in H2O

Leatherbacks are the largest sea turtles. They eat jellies and dive deep like whales.

MAMA & BABY HUMPBACK WHALES

LEATHERBACK

Kemp's Ridley sea turtles eat crabs, clams and snails. They are the rarest and most endangered.

KEMP'S RIDLEY TURTLE

Olive Ridley Turtles are olive green. They swim along ancient drift lines where there are masses of floating seaweed. And they feed on the animals that live in the seaweed. Crabs, jellies, clams, snails and some algae are their preferences.

Olive Ridley eating a Jelly lunch

Green Sea Turtles are gentle herbivores. They eat sea grasses and rooted algae which gives them a greenish color. So beautiful!

Sea Stars & Yummy Sea Grass

GREEN SEA TURTLE

13

Hawksbill turtles live along coral reefs and eat sponges. They have a strongly hooked beak. Gotta have one. Their shells are dark amber, brown and black with whitish-yellow streaks. The beautiful markings are to die for. Try snorkeling in a coral reef, it's amazing.

CORAL REEF

BABY HAWKSBILL TURTLE

Loggerhead turtles have very large heads. They feed along the water column in shallows, eating horseshoe crabs. They eat in estuaries along the continental shelf and also in the open ocean. As well as crabs, they like eating clams, sea snails, sea pens and an assortment of invertebrates. We haven't even gotten to the good stuff yet.

LOGGERHEAD TURTLE BY MELENA, 7 YEARS OLD WITH ASSIST

Flatback turtles live in Australia and avoid jaggedy reefs because they have a soft shell. They like to eat jellies and soft bodied invertebrates in soft shallow waters. Avoiding reefs makes perfect sense, but only in this case.

FLATBACK TURTLE IN THE SHALLOWS

I consider the good stuff as talking about the mamas and their eggs and babies. And now we get to talk about the good stuff.

Female sea turtles are sometimes 35 years old before laying their first batch of eggs. They nest on the beaches when the moon is just right and miraculously—it is the same place where they were hatched.

The mothers go into a trance and nothing can interrupt their motherly instinct when it's time to dig a hole in the sand and put the next generation in the sand. These mamas are on a mission.

It is important that <u>our</u> next generation sees <u>their</u> next generation populating the oceans of earth. And I trust that God will raise up those in each generation to carry on authentic nurturing of these ancient swimmers. I pray there will be godly people for generations to come who will carry God's love and truth to all future generations.

There is a world of possibilities in every seed of life.

In the Mediterranean Sea, Loggerheads and red coral are both endangered.

"Ridin' along in my automobile."
Greens love riding the currents
of the deep blue oceans.

GREEN IN THE DEEP BLUE

The babies are super cute. They are called hatchlings.
"I'm on my way to success."

Baby sea turtles are not seen with their mothers. Instead they go off on their own drifting along, riding the currents, gulf stream and straights around the entire earth. Sometimes the babies are never seen again until they are much older. Each generation needs our care. Possibly a 7 year old student of mine like Malena will grow up to take care of creatures like these. We can raise awareness in our children.

Draw me away Jesus, and we will sail the deep blue ocean of life.

This mama is on a mission to lay eggs in the sand. In many cases, it is the same exact place where she was hatched.

Children like Malena do sea turtle art and it makes them love these creatures.

These cute little cleaner fish give the turtles a good once over at a cleaning station. "I'll have a clean and shine please! You can have a meal, it's on me."

God created all the life and creatures in the cosmos, both in water, land and space. You and I are the pinnacle of His creation...His most prized work of art. You are a unique, one-of-a-kind, valued masterpiece.

Let your soul prosper by seeking the Face of God. Talk, walk with and follow Him everywhere you go. When your soul is prospering and your being is in good health, then you can do your part to help the creatures on the planet.

Julie Seuss[2] shares with us how to do our part to help Sea Turtles:
1. Help out by not buying Tortoise shell items like brushes, eye glasses, furniture or ornaments.
2. Keep the beaches clean.

---

[2] Julie Seuss of Julie Seuss Photography is a photographer of Sea Turtles underwater and on land. She is on Face Book and Instagram under Julie Seuss Photography. See her videos and photos of Sea Turtles in the wild. Julie is an advocate and lover of these beautiful creatures. Learn more by visiting her on Face Book.

3. Reduce your use of plastic particularly single use plastic such as straws, plastic bottles and plastic utensils.
4. Do not let balloons go.
5. Never disturb nesting turtles or their nests, eggs or hatchlings.
6. Never use flash photography (this can cause the turtle to abandon the nesting process).
7. Always help do your best to keep the beaches clean, dark and flat.

Thanks Julie.

Jo Earlam is a Sea Turtle advocate from the UK. She has written a book called , Tuamor the Turtle[3]. It focuses on the dangers of plastic pollution to Sea Turtles. Tuamor means "love you".

"People protect what they love." Jacques Yves Cousteau

---

[3] Tuamor the Turtle on Face Book and tuamoretheturtle.com.

Jo Earlam speaks to children about the Sea Turtle's plight on planet earth. She helps in beach cleaning projects. You will learn a lot from her. You may one day help in a beach cleaning project yourself, or even teach others about Sea Turtles.

About the Art

All of the art in this book is done by Deana G. Harvey and is available for sale in original, print or commission. Call for permission to use any art in this book 260-402-7951. © Deana G. Harvey

Other Books Written and Illustrated by Deana G. Harvey:
Genesis One, The Story of Creation, CreateSpace 2013
The Tree of Life, It Comes Natural for a Tree, CreateSpace 2013
Petie the Pecock, Eyes All Around, CreateSpace 2016
All are available through Amazon.com or call 260-402-7951

Face book: Deana Artist Tree of Life Gallery, Roanoke IN
Face book personal page: Deana Harvey
Instagram: Deana Tree of Life
Tree of Life Art Gallery by Deana Harvey & Vintage Clothing Store by Emily Shilts: located at 331 N. Main Street, Roanoke, IN. Call 260-402-7951 to check for open hours.
Website: Deana Artist for God at WIX.com
Page No. and Details

P.3 Detail of Sea Star, Blue Tang and Flame Wrasse, 36x48x2", Acrylic & Molding Paste on Canvas

p.4 8x10" Watercolor on paper

p.5 Zero Gravity, 8x10", Oil on Canvas

p.6 Mama & Baby Humpback Whales, 18x24x3/4", Oil on canvas

p.7 Leatherback, 8.5x11", Watercolor Collage' with Origami Paper

p.8 Prism Waterfall, 24x36", Acrylic on Canvas

p.9 Kemps Ridley Turtle, 8x11", Watercolor and salt on Paper

p.10 Mediterranean Sea Star & Clams, 12x12" Watercolor on Paper

p.11 Olive Ridley 18x24", Acrylic on Canvas

p.12 Sea Stars & Sea Grass, 8x10", Watercolor & Salt on Paper

p.13 Green Sea Turtle, 18x24", Acrylic with Molding Paste

p.14 Coral Reef, 8x10", Watercolor on Paper

p.15 Baby Hawksbill, 5x7", Watercolor Paper

p.16 Loggerhead, 10x10", Acrylic on Canvas with Glitter by Malena, 7 year old student with assist from Deana Harvey.

p.17 Same as p.16

p.18 Abstract, 8x10", Watercolor on paper

p.19 Flatback in the Shallows, 18x24", Acrylic with Molding, Sea Shells & Silver Leaf on Canvas

p.21 Seeds of Life, 18x24", Oil on Canvas

p.22 Loggerhead & Red Coral, 11x14", Acrylic under painted, with Oils, Glitter & Glass Beads as the top layer

p.24 Green in the Deep Blue, 14x14", Acrylic on Canvas

p.25 Baby Loggerhead, 8x10", Watercolor & Pen on Paper

p.26 Mama& Baby, 36x48x2", Acrylic with Molding Paste

p.27 Draw Me Away Jesus, Diptych, Acrylic on 2 canvases 8x24" each

p.28 Same as p.19

P.29 Same as p. 16

p.30 Cleaning Station, 8xll", Watercolor & Salt on Paper

p.36 Sea Turtle and Sea Stars, 18x24", Mixed Media & Acrylic on Canvas

Secure the future generations. Mission accomplished!

On the following pages, draw or color pictures of Sea Turtles, Sea Turtle Eggs or Sea Turtle Hatchlings.

Deana G. Harvey